JOHN THOMPSON'S
EASIEST PIANO COURSE

FIRST CLASSICAL DUETS

Arranged by Eric Baumgartner

ISBN 978-1-70511-231-1

Willis Music

EXCLUSIVELY DISTRIBUTED BY

HAL•LEONARD®

Visit Hal Leonard Online at
www.halleonard.com

Contact us:
Hal Leonard
7777 West Bluemound Road
Milwaukee, WI 53213
Email: info@halleonard.com

In Europe, contact:
Hal Leonard Europe Limited
42 Wigmore Street
Marylebone, London, W1U 2RN
Email: info@halleonardeurope.com

In Australia, contact:
Hal Leonard Australia Pty. Ltd.
4 Lentara Court
Cheltenham, Victoria, 3192 Australia
Email: info@halleonard.com.au

Teachers and Parents

This collection of classical duets, arranged in the John Thompson tradition, is intended as supplementary material for advancing young pianists in the Easiest Piano Course. Listed in the suggested order of study, most students can begin playing the simpler arrangements after Part 2, and the difficulty level progresses through to Part 4. The pieces may also be used for sight-reading practice by more advanced students.

Spring

from *The Four Seasons*

SECONDO

Antonio Vivaldi
Arranged by Eric Baumgartner

Briskly, joyfully

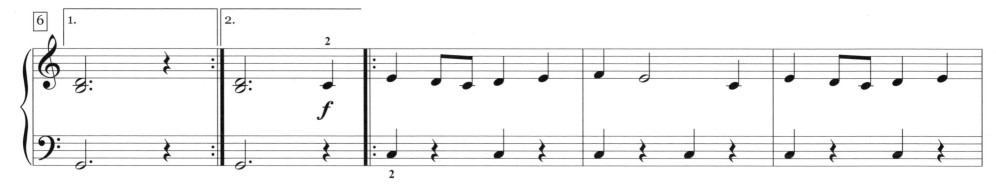

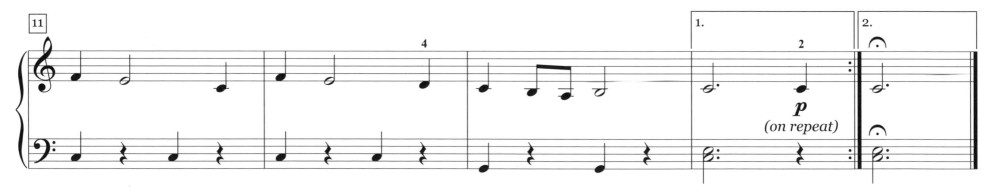

Spring
from *The Four Seasons*

PRIMO

Antonio Vivaldi
Arranged by Eric Baumgartner

Briskly, joyfully

Ode to Joy

SECONDO

Ludwig van Beethoven
Arranged by Eric Baumgartner

Ode to Joy

PRIMO

Ludwig van Beethoven
Arranged by Eric Baumgartner

Minuet in G Major

SECONDO

Christian Petzold
Arranged by Eric Baumgartner

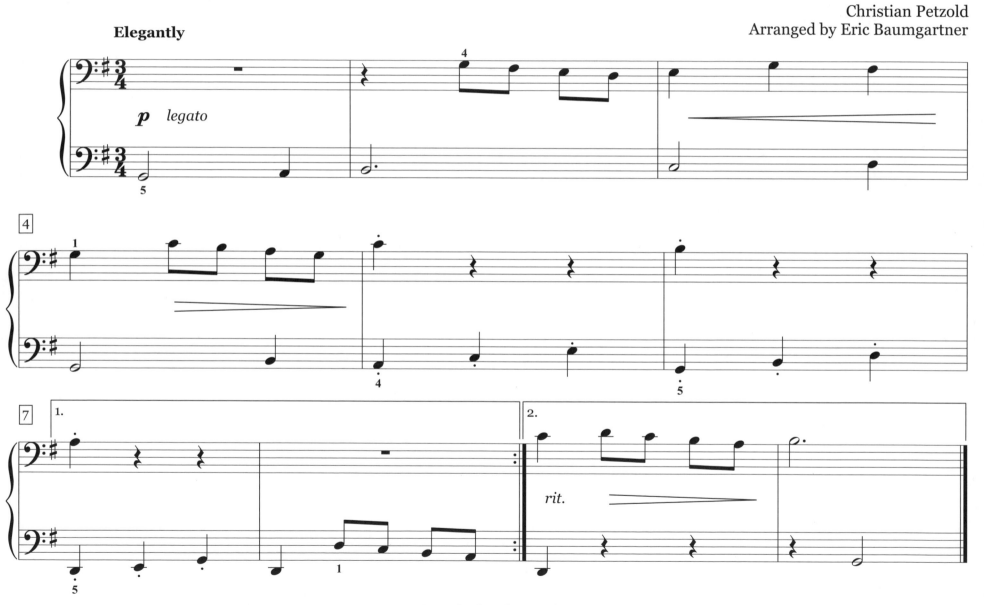

Minuet in G Major

PRIMO

Christian Petzold
Arranged by Eric Baumgartner

L.H. over

Rondeau

SECONDO

Jean-Joseph Mouret
Arranged by Eric Baumgartner

Majestic march tempo

Rondeau

PRIMO

Jean-Joseph Mouret
Arranged by Eric Baumgartner

Barcarolle

SECONDO

Jacques Offenbach
Arranged by Eric Baumgartner

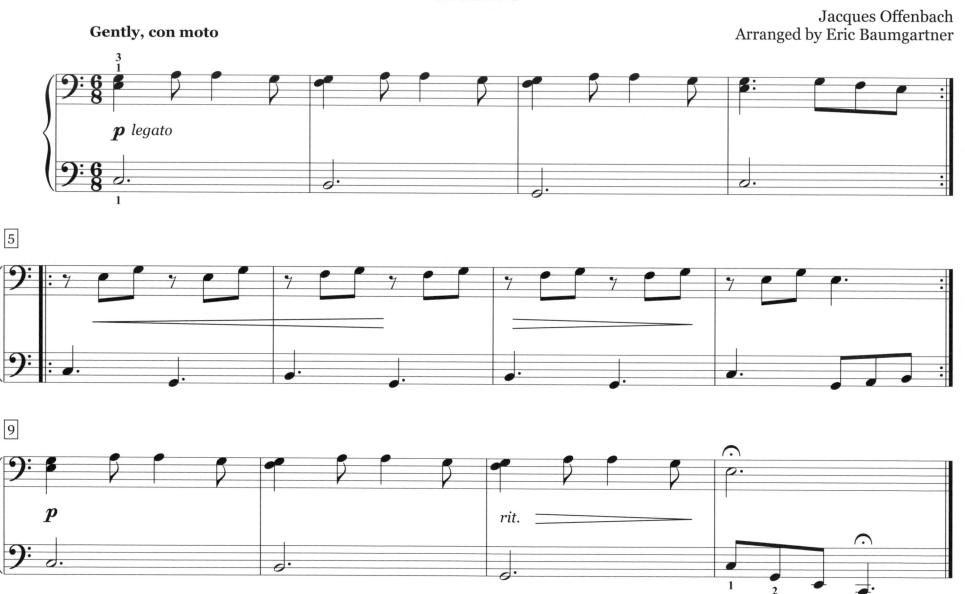

Barcarolle

PRIMO

Jacques Offenbach
Arranged by Eric Baumgartner

Piano Concerto No. 1

1st Movement

SECONDO

Pyotr Il'yich Tchaikovsky
Arranged by Eric Baumgartner

Piano Concerto No. 1

1st Movement

PRIMO

Pyotr Il'yich Tchaikovsky
Arranged by Eric Baumgartner

SECONDO

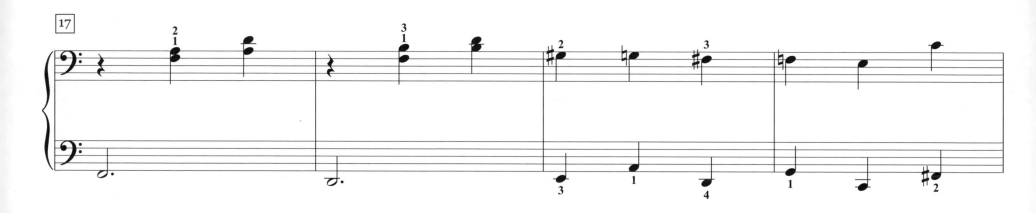

PRIMO

Symphony No. 5

1st Movement

SECONDO

Ludwig van Beethoven
Arranged by Eric Baumgartner

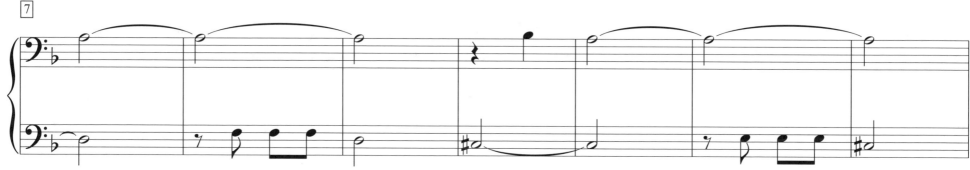

Symphony No. 5

1st Movement

PRIMO

Ludwig van Beethoven
Arranged by Eric Baumgartner

SECONDO

PRIMO

New World Symphony

4th Movement

SECONDO

Antonín Dvořák
Arranged by Eric Baumgartner

New World Symphony
4th Movement
PRIMO

Antonín Dvořák
Arranged by Eric Baumgartner

Allegro, dramatically
R.H. 8va throughout

In the Hall of the Mountain King

SECONDO

Edvard Grieg
Arranged by Eric Baumgartner

Sprightly, but not too fast

In the Hall of the Mountain King

PRIMO

Edvard Grieg
Arranged by Eric Baumgartner

The Swan

SECONDO

Camille Saint-Saëns
Arranged by Eric Baumgartner

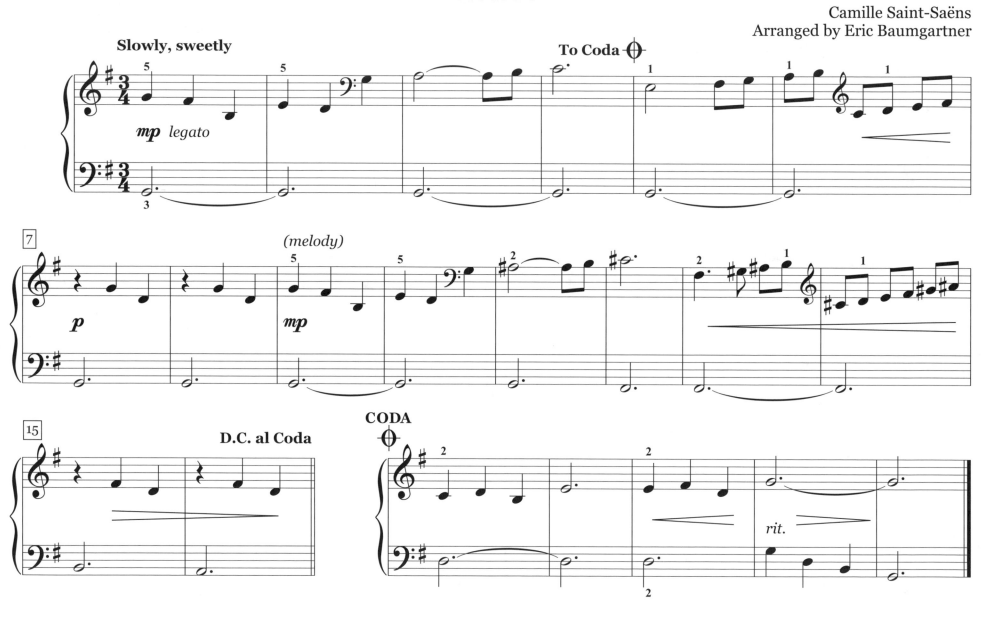

The Swan

PRIMO

Camille Saint-Saëns
Arranged by Eric Baumgartner

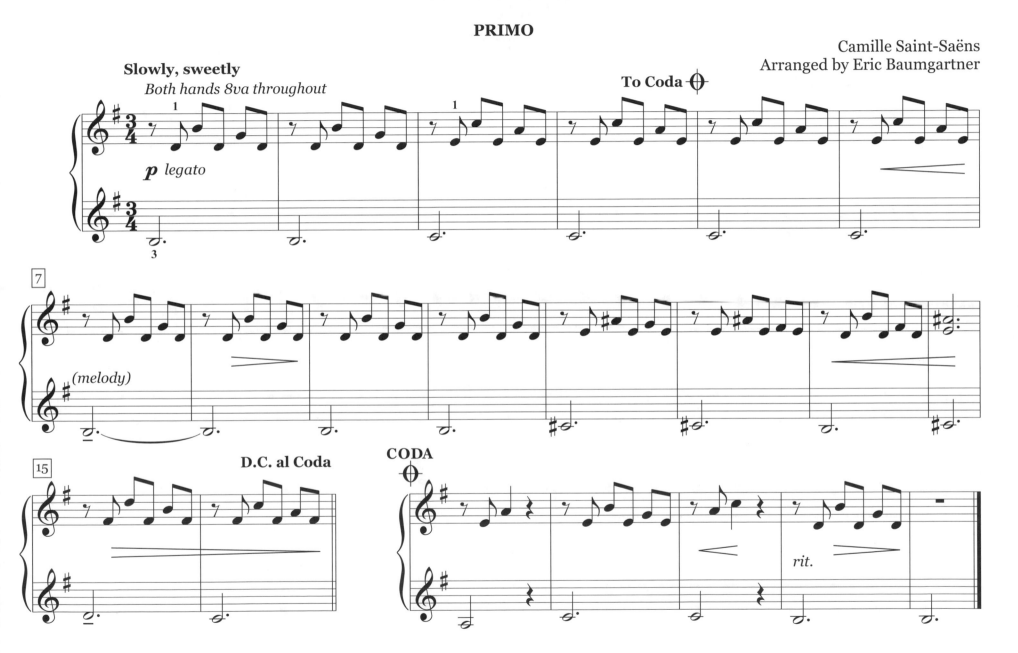

Eine Kleine Nachtmusik
1st Movement

SECONDO

Wolfgang Amadeus Mozart
Arranged by Eric Baumgartner

Eine Kleine Nachtmusik
1st Movement

PRIMO

Wolfgang Amadeus Mozart
Arranged by Eric Baumgartner

Briskly, with energy

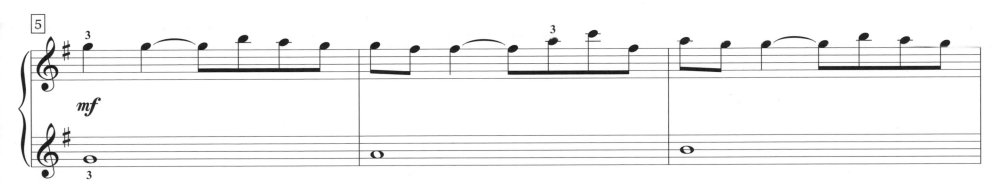

SECONDO

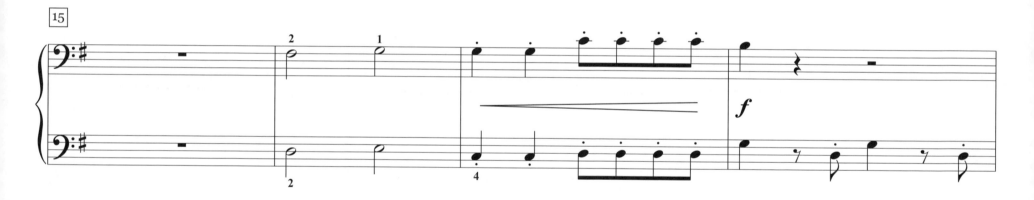

PRIMO

EASIEST PIANO COURSE
Supplementary Songbooks

Fun repertoire books are available as an integral part of **John Thompson's Easiest Piano Course**. Graded to work alongside the course, these pieces are ideal for pupils reaching the end of Part 2. They are invaluable for securing basic technique as well as developing musicality and enjoyment.

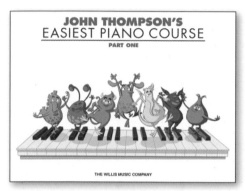

John Thompson's Easiest Piano Course

00414014	Part 1 – Book only	$6.99
00414018	Part 2 – Book only	$6.99
00414019	Part 3 – Book only	$7.99
00414112	Part 4 – Book only	$7.99

First Beethoven *arr. Hussey*
00171709 .... $7.99

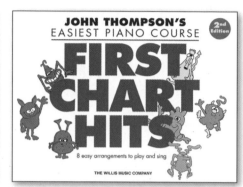

First Chart Hits – 2nd Edition
00289560 .... $9.99

First Disney Songs *arr. Miller*
00416880 .... $9.99

Also available:

First Children's Songs *arr. Hussey*
00282895 .... $7.99

First Classics
00406347 .... $6.99

First Disney Favorites *arr. Hussey*
00319587 .... $9.99

First Mozart *arr. Hussey*
00171851 .... $7.99

First Nursery Rhymes
00406229 .... $6.99

First Worship Songs *arr. Austin*
00416892 .... $8.99

First Jazz Tunes *arr. Baumgartner*
00120872 .... $7.99

First Pop Songs *arr. Miller*
00416954 .... $8.99

First Showtunes *arr. Hussey*
00282907 .... $9.99